Hot, Hotter, Hottest

Animals That Adapt to Great Heat

by Michael Dahl

illustrated by Brian Jensen

PICTURE WINDOW BOOKS
Minneapolis, Minnesota

Thanks to our advisers for their expertise, research, and advice:

Dr. James F. Hare, Associate Professor of Zoology
University of Manitoba
Winnipeg, Manitoba

Susan Kesselring, M.A., Literacy Educator
Rosemount-Apple Valley-Eagan (Minnesota) School District

Editorial Director: Carol Jones
Managing Editor: Catherine Neitge
Creative Director: Keith Griffin
Editor: Christianne Jones
Story Consultant: Terry Flaherty
Designer: Nathan Gassman
Production Artist: Angela Kilmer
Page Production: Picture Window Books
The illustrations in this book were created with pastels.

Picture Window Books
5115 Excelsior Boulevard, Suite 232
Minneapolis, MN 55416
877-845-8392
www.picturewindowbooks.com

Printed in the United States of America.

Library of Congress Cataloging-in-Publication Data
Dahl, Michael.
Hot, hotter, hottest : animals that adapt to great heat /
written by Michael Dahl ; illustrated by Brian Jensen.
p. cm. — (Animal extremes)
Includes bibliographical references and index.
ISBN 1-4048-1017-X (hardcover)
1. Heat adaptation—Juvenile literature. I. Jensen, Brian, ill.
II. Title.

QH543.2.D344 2005
591.4'2—dc22   2005003735

The red-spotted toad can!
...wls beneath rocks to
...rom the 90° F
...n Mexico.

Animals live everywhere. They fly over the highest mountains and swim in the deepest oceans. They run over the hottest deserts and dive into the coldest waters.

Try to stay cool as you read about animals that survive extreme heat. Watch the numbers on the thermometer rise as you turn each page.

3

Pft-pft-pft-pft

A monarch butterfly flies through many different temperatures on its way to Mexico for the winter. It survives 88° F.

Can any animal exist in a hotter climate?

°F

160 —

140 —

120 —

100 —

80 —
88° Fahrenheit
31° Celsius

60 —

40 —

20 —

0 —

-20 —

-40 —

-60 —

°F
160
140
120
100
90° Fahrenheit
32° Celsius
80
60
40
20
0
-20
-40
-60

°C
70
60
50
40
30
20
10
0
-10
-20
-30
-40
-50

Can any animal exist in a hotter climate?

Yes! The fennec fox can! It only leaves its burrow in northern Africa at night. It survives 95° F.

Can any animal exist in a hotter climate?

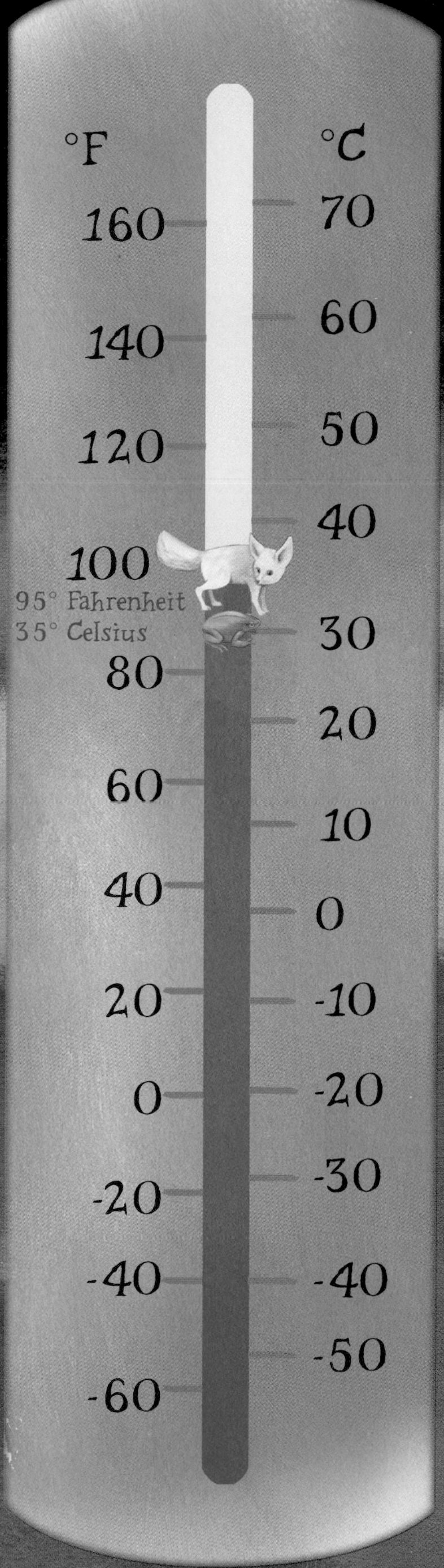

°F

160

140

120

100
95° Fahrenheit
35° Celsius

80

60

40

20

0

-20

-40

-60

°C

70

60

50

40

30

20

10

0

-10

-20

-30

-40

-50

Yes! The burrowing owl can! It survives 98° F as it stands guard over its home in Mexico.

Can any animal exist in a hotter climate?

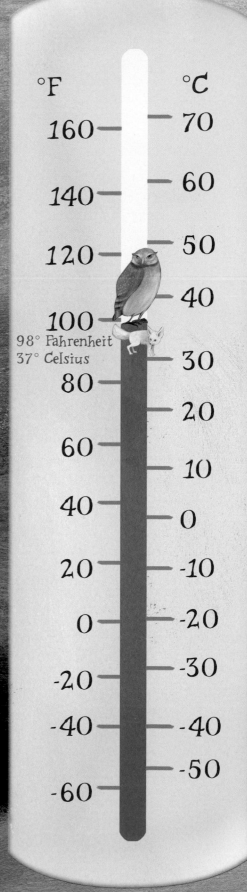

°F

160—
140—
120—
100—
98° Fahrenheit
37° Celsius
80—
60—
40—
20—
0—
-20—
-40—
-60—

°C

—70
—60
—50
—40
—30
—20
—10
—0
—-10
—-20
—-30
—-40
—-50

Yes! The antelope jackrabbit can! It sits in the cool shade of a cactus in the Sonoran Desert in Arizona. It survives 100° F.

Can any animal exist in a hotter climate?

A monarch butterfly flies through many different temperatures on its way to Mexico for the winter. It survives 88° F.

Can any animal exist in a hotter climate?

°F

160
140
120
100
80
88° Fahrenheit
31° Celsius
60
40
20
0
-20
-40
-60

°C

70
60
50
40
30
20
10
0
-10
-20
-30
-40
-50

Yes! The red-spotted toad can!
It crawls beneath rocks to
hide from the 90° F
heat in Mexico.

6

Pft-pft-pft-pft

Animals live everywhere. They fly over the highest mountains and swim in the deepest oceans. They run over the hottest deserts and dive into the coldest waters.

Try to stay cool as you read about animals that survive extreme heat. Watch the numbers on the thermometer rise as you turn each page.

Can any animal exist in a hotter climate?

°F
160
140
120
100
90° Fahrenheit
32° Celsius
80
60
40
20
0
-20
-40
-60

°C
70
60
50
40
30
20
10
0
-10
-20
-30
-40
-50

Yes! The fennec fox can! It only leaves its burrow in northern Africa at night. It survives 95° F.

8

Can any animal exist in a hotter climate?

°F
160
140
120
100
95° Fahrenheit
35° Celsius
80
60
40
20
0
-20
-40
-60

°C
70
60
50
40
30
20
10
0
-10
-20
-30
-40
-50

Yes! The burrowing owl can! It survives 98° F as it stands guard over its home in Mexico.

Can any animal exist
in a hotter climate?

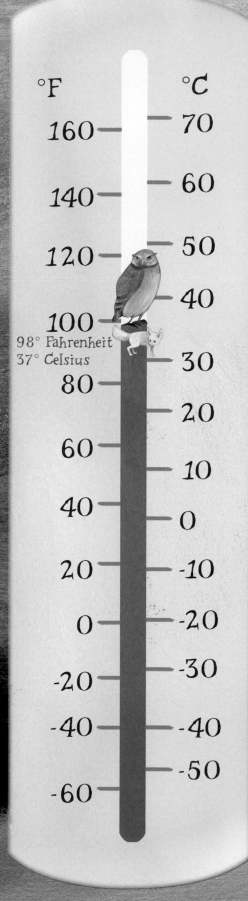

°F

160—

140—

120—

100—
98° Fahrenheit
37° Celsius
80—

60—

40—

20—

0—

-20—

-40—

-60—

°C

—70

—60

—50

—40

—30

—20

—10

—0

—-10

—-20

—-30

—-40

—-50

Yes! The antelope jackrabbit can! It sits in the cool shade of a cactus in the Sonoran Desert in Arizona. It survives 100° F.

Can any animal exist in a hotter climate?

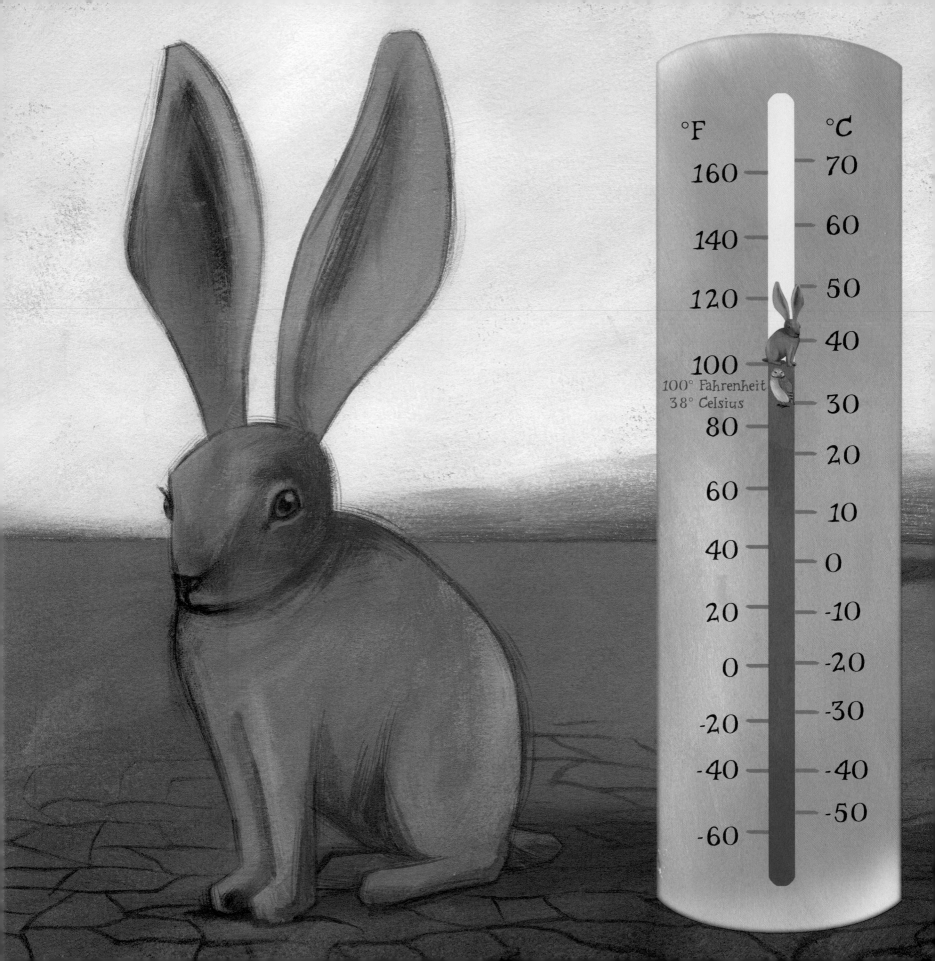

°F

160

140

120

100
100° Fahrenheit
38° Celsius

80

60

40

20

0

-20

-40

-60

°C

70

60

50

40

30

20

10

0

-10

-20

-30

-40

-50

Yes! A long-tailed pocket mouse can! During the day, it burrows to survive 115° F heat of the Mojave Desert.

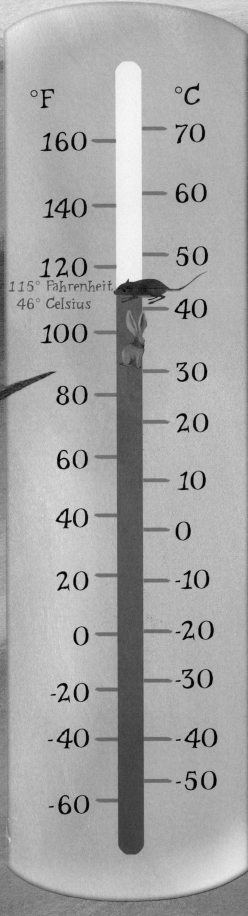

Yes! The male Bactrian camel can! It survives 140° F. It grinds its teeth and puffs its cheeks to attract a mate in the Gobi Desert.

Can any animal exist in a hotter climate?

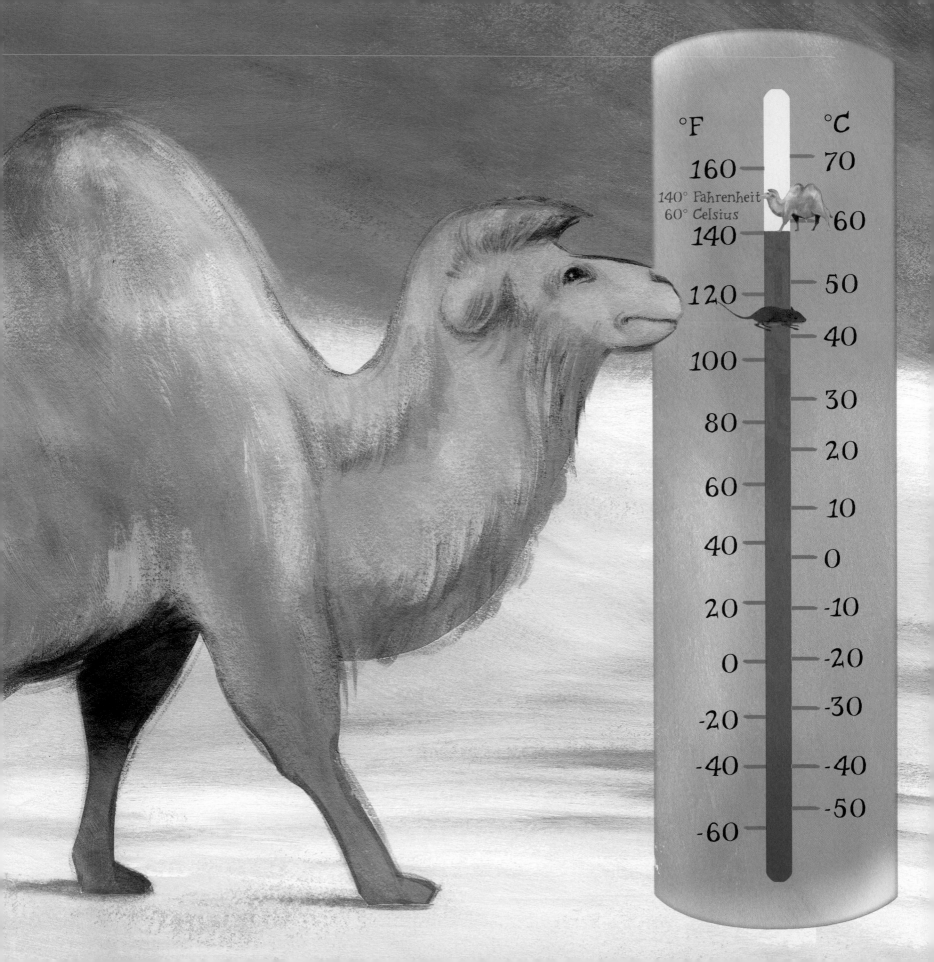

°F
160
140° Fahrenheit
60° Celsius
140
120
100
80
60
40
20
0
-20
-40
-60

°C
70
60
50
40
30
20
10
0
-10
-20
-30
-40
-50

Yes! The Pompeii worm can! It slides inside its tube deep in the Pacific Ocean to hide from the hot gas of a hydrothermal vent. It survives temperatures of 176° F.

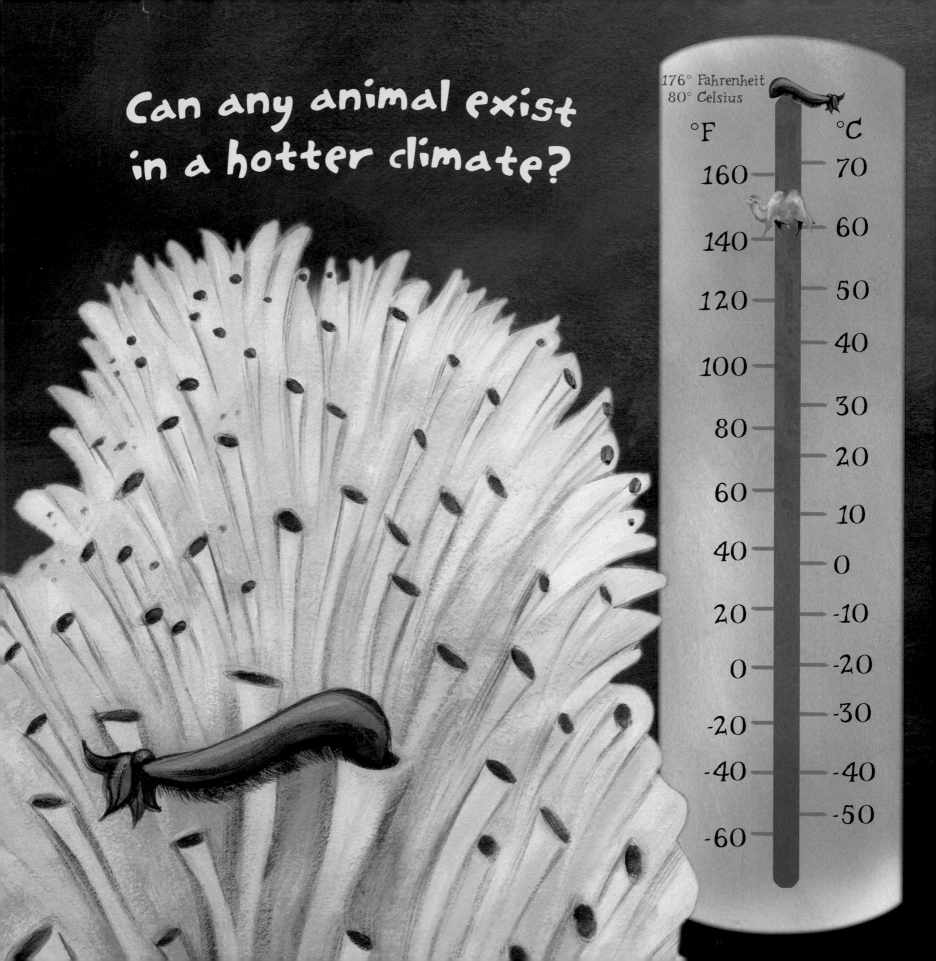

20

Perhaps. Who knows what could exist in hotter climates?

Extreme Fun

The most heat-tolerant animal known on Earth is the Pompeii worm.

Pompeii worm

A Bactrian camel can go several weeks without any water.

Bactrian camel

The long-tailed pocket mouse does not drink water. It gets its water from the green plants it eats.

long-tailed pocket mouse

Antelope jackrabbits use their long ears to cool off. Their body heat escapes through blood vessels close to the skin in their ears.

antelope jackrabbit

The burrowing owl is often called the ground owl because it makes its nest underground instead of in trees.

burrowing owl

Facts

The fennec fox has fur on the bottom of its feet to help protect it from hot sand.

The color of a red-spotted toad often matches its background. No matter what color the toad is, it always has little red bumps.

While migrating, the monarch butterfly can cover 80 miles (128 kilometers) a day! The longest recorded flight of a monarch butterfly is more than 3,000 miles (4,800 kilometers).

fennec fox

red-spotted toad

monarch butterfly

Glossary

burrow—a hole or tunnel in the ground made by an animal, usually for its home

cactus—a plant covered in spines that is found in desert areas

grind—to press down and rub

hydrothermal vent—a hole on the ocean floor that releases extremely hot water

migrating—to travel regularly from one place to another in autumn and spring

protect—to keep safe from danger

survive—to stay alive

thermometer—a tool for measuring temperature

tolerant—ability to put up with something

To Learn More

At the Library

Auch, Alison. *Desert Animals.* Minneapolis: Compass Point Books, 2003.

Butterfield, Moira. *Animals in Hot Places.* Austin, Texas: Raintree Steck and Vaughn, 2000.

Hoff, Mary King. *Handling Heat.* Mankato, Minn.: Creative Education, 2003.

On the Web

FactHound offers a safe, fun way to find Web sites related to this book. All of the sites on FactHound have been researched by our staff.

www.facthound.com

1. Visit the FactHound home page.

2. Enter a search word related to this book, or type in this special code: 140481017X

3. Click on the FETCH IT button.

Your trusty FactHound will fetch the best sites for you!

Look for all of the books in the Animal Extremes series:

Cold, Colder, Coldest: *Animals That Adapt to Cold Weather*

Deep, Deeper, Deepest: *Animals That Go to Great Depths*

Fast, Faster, Fastest: *Animals That Move at Great Speeds*

High, Higher, Highest: *Animals That Go to Great Heights*

Hot, Hotter, Hottest: *Animals That Adapt to Great Heat*

Old, Older, Oldest: *Animals That Live Long Lives*